MY HOLI
Colors of Cheer

by
Priya Kumari
Komal Garg

Eternal Tree Books

art by
Abhilasha Khatri

Mother Nature looks so happy. Bright marigolds, green henna leaves, vibrant hibiscuses, fragrant roses, and orange *palash* flowers are welcoming spring.

Aadi and Leela are excited to make colors to play Holi. They have come to the Himalayan foothills to meet their grandparents and celebrate Holi with them.

"It seems so many leaves and flowers bloom for us to play Holi," exclaims Leela.

"Not only flowers and leaves, Mother Nature also gives us food to eat," says Grandpa. "Today, on Chhoti Holi we also thank her for the harvest to come."

"Are we going to meet Maaloo?" Papa asks Grandpa.

"Who is Maaloo?" asks Aadi.

"He is our family friend and a farmer. When I was a kid, I learned many things about farming from him," tells Papa. "Farmers work hard sowing, weeding, irrigating, and harvesting so people can have food. They turn soil into food for us."

"They are like Food Magicians!" adds Grandpa.

"Yes. Holi is also a festival of celebrating good harvest," continues Papa, "isn't it great to go thank a farmer for their hard work?"

"That will be so exciting," cheers Leela as they leave to meet Maaloo.

Soon they reach Maaloo's farm. The farm is full of wheat which will soon be ready for harvest. Maaloo is incredibly happy to see them.

He gifts them a small bunch of wheat for Holika Dahan. Grandpa also invites Maaloo and his family for Holika Dahan in the evening.

"Do you want a ride on the tractor?" offers Maaloo.

"Absolutely!" Aadi and Leela are delighted to experience a few moments of a farmer's life.

"IT'S TIME...Let's all go for Holika Dahan," says Grandma.

"Yayyy!" Aadi and Leela hurry to join the event.

Families gather and build a huge bonfire, *Holi*. They offer coconuts, *upalas*, and turmeric to it. Grandpa and his friends light the bonfire and everyone walks around it. They also offer wheat corns to the god of fire, *Agni*. "The first crop before the harvest is offered to gods and we thank gods for a good harvest," Farmer Maaloo arrives.

Papa ties a small wheat bunch onto a staff and roasts it in the fire. The wheat corns turn sweet! Maa asks Aadi and Leela to share *prasad* of sweet wheat corns and cooked coconut with Uncle Maaloo.

For some time, they all stand near the fire. "It feels so refreshing," says Leela.

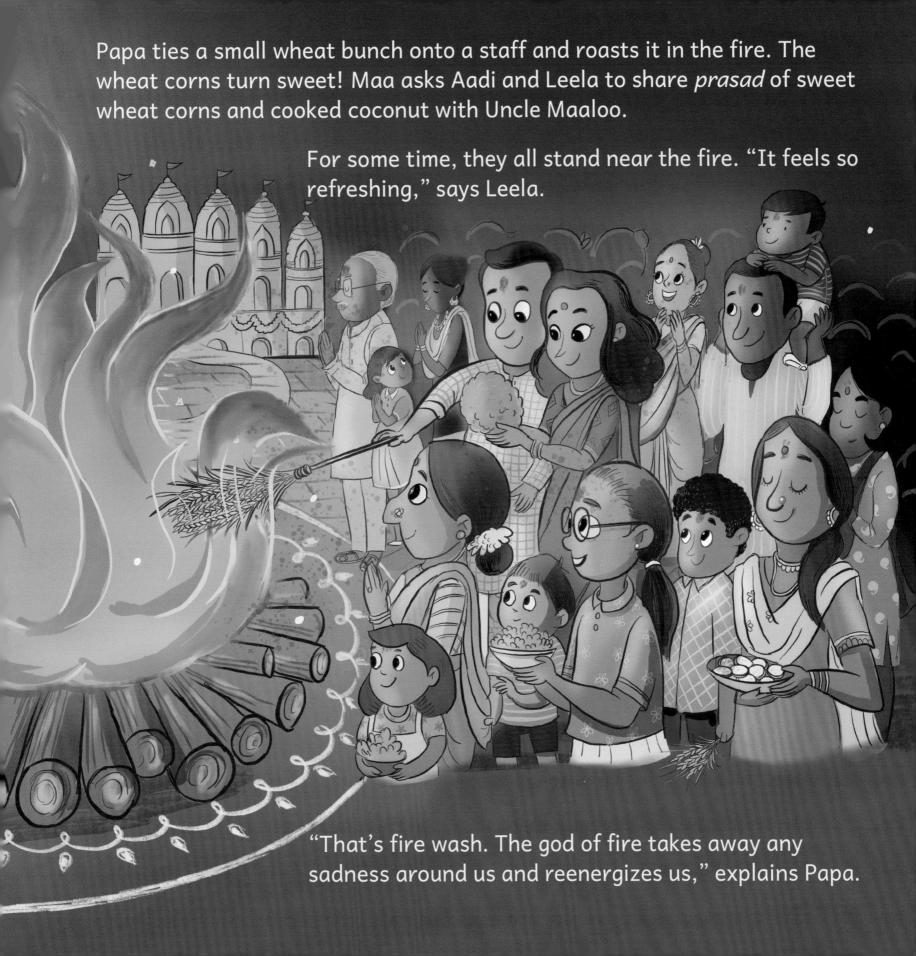

"That's fire wash. The god of fire takes away any sadness around us and reenergizes us," explains Papa.

Today is Badi Holi, the main day when people play with colors. Many friends and cousins come to play Holi.

Leela comes with her *pichkari* and drenches Aadi with colored water.

"Ha! Wait for me you little munchkin! I'll get you!"
Aadi runs to get his pichkari.

The beating of drums and dancing make the play more fun. Maa and her friends sing folksongs to cherish the playful childhood of Radha and Krishna. Aadi and Leela laugh, play, and dance with friends and family through the afternoon until everyone is out of colors and balloons!

In the evening, they visit Aunt Meena and Uncle Jay to wish them a happy Holi.

Everyone enjoys moon shaped *gujiyas*, spicy *dahi vadas*, and cool *thandai*.

After the fun-filled day, they come back home. Aadi and Leela have a question, "Papa, why do we celebrate Holi?"

"Let me tell you the story of Bhakta Prahlad, his father, Hiranya-Kashipu, and his evil aunt, Holika," says Papa.

"Hiranya-Kashipu was a powerful evil king. He was misusing his powers against innocent people. He was so madly arrogant that he did not respect the light of life in all beings and things, represented by Lord Vishnu. He wanted everyone to worship him out of fear of being killed. He did not allow anyone to exercise their free will and worship Lord Vishnu."

"That's not fair, Papa. How can anyone force people to believe something out of fear?" grumbles Aadi.

"When there was a rule of such fear, his son was born. His name was Prahlad. The boy was born with a questioning mind and saw the presence of gods in all beings and things. Meaning he was devoted to Lord Vishnu," says Papa.

Leela is so curious to know more about Prahlad.

"The evil king did not like this. He sent a mad elephant to kill Prahlad but the boy survived. His soldiers threw Prahlad off a cliff but magically the boy landed safely on a flower. Multiple such attempts failed as a divine light saved the little boy every time."

"At last, the enraged king went to his sister, Holika. She had a special power —fire could not burn her. 'You sit in fire with Prahlad. The little devotee of Vishnu will burn but you will be safe,' said the demon king."

"As fire soared, it destroyed Holika but Prahlad survived! In her mad rush to destroy Prahlad, Holika misused her power and the god of fire destroyed her."

"Papa! What happened to the evil king? Did he realize his mistake?" asks Aadi.

"No, he did not. He had a special power. *Devas*, humans, or animals could not punish him. He could not be defeated during day or night. No one could fight him either inside or outside his palace and no weapon could stop him," says Papa.

"But it was so important to stop him from torturing innocent people, Papa. What happened then?" Leela feels anxious.

"Seeing Prahlad's devotion for Lord Vishnu, the frustrated king asked, 'Where is your Vishnu?'

'He is everywhere,' said Prahlad.

'Is he present in this pillar?' asked the king.

Prahlad nodded, and it made his father so angry that he took out his sword to break the pillar. And then, there was a loud roar!"

"To stop evil deeds and protect Prahlad, Lord Vishnu appeared at twilight—neither day nor night—as a lion-headed man—neither human nor animal. It's the fiercest avatar of the Lord—Narsimha, that was necessary to bring peace. Narsimha sat on the threshold—neither inside nor outside—and put the demon on his lap and tore him with his nails—no weapons were used."

"Prahlad ruled the kingdom with wisdom and kindness, thereafter. Since then, Holika Dahan is performed as a symbol of destroying evil deeds and crime," says Papa.

"And, why did we walk around the Holi fire yesterday?" asks Leela.

"Let me tell you the story of Dhondha," joins Maa. "Once, Yudhishthira asked Lord Krishna, 'Lord! Why do we light fire on Holi?' Lord Krishna relates the story of King Raghu, who always followed the path of *Dharma*. Once, his subjects complained, 'O King! Dhondha is causing great suffering to our children. Please help!' The king asked his guru for advice."

"What did the guru say?" asks Leela.

Sandalwood

Sesame & Mustard Seeds

Cow dung cakes

Camphor

Cardamom

"'Dhondha has such a power that no weapons can defeat her. She cannot be defeated in hot, cold, or rainy weather. But when two seasons meet, joyfulness can disempower her. To defeat her, everyone should enjoy, dance, say funny things, and laugh. Children should carry wooden swords in their hands as if they are battle-ready. Medicinal substances should be collected and offered into fire. Everyone should take three rounds of fire. This can destroy the demoness,' advised the guru. The demoness here refers to illnesses due to weather change. The fire ritual protects us from illnesses," tells Maa.

"Also, there was a demoness, Putna, who was sent by Kansa to kill baby Krishna. She magically turned into a very pretty lady and took Krishna into her lap to feed him poisonous milk."

"Baby Krishna was brave enough to destroy her. Her effigy is also burnt by many people on Holi," adds Papa.

"WOW! Now I know. Holi inspires us to be playful, joyful, brave, and healthy," says the thoughtful Aadi.

"Yes! Exactly!" agrees Papa.

"Holi is such an important festival that it is celebrated in many interesting ways across India," continues Maa.

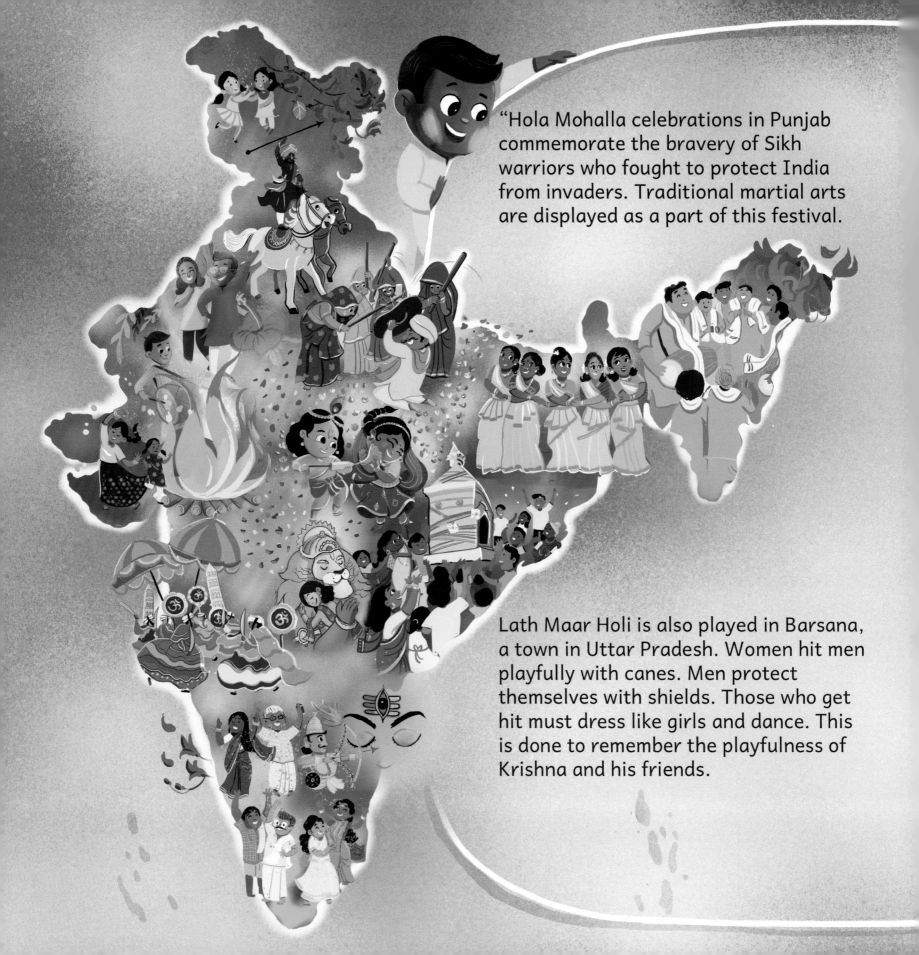

"Hola Mohalla celebrations in Punjab commemorate the bravery of Sikh warriors who fought to protect India from invaders. Traditional martial arts are displayed as a part of this festival.

Lath Maar Holi is also played in Barsana, a town in Uttar Pradesh. Women hit men playfully with canes. Men protect themselves with shields. Those who get hit must dress like girls and dance. This is done to remember the playfulness of Krishna and his friends.

Holi is played with fresh flowers in many places, especially in Vrindavan where Lord Krishna spent his childhood. It is called Phulon ki Holi.

In West Bengal and Odisha it is known as Dola Poornima and Dol Yatra. Devotees carry beautifully adorned palanquins of Lord Krishna across cities. They play with colors, dance, and sing in the memory of Lord Krishna.

It is called Yaosang festival in Manipur. Special folk dance of Manipur, Thanbal Chongba, is performed along with the play of wet and dry colors.

Shigmo street dances are performed, and traditional folk songs are sung by farmers in the region of Goa.

Kaman pandikai is celebrated in Tamil Nadu. Kama Deva and his wife Rati are worshipped on this day for their sacrifice which was needed to destroy an invincible demon. This is also called Madan-Mahotsava and Kama-Dahanam in other regions.

In Kerala, Holi is played with turmeric and is called Manjal Kuli (turmeric bath) or ukali.

The festival has many more names and is celebrated across India and by many across the globe. It is a festival to enjoy colors of goodness, justice, playfulness, love, friendship, and most importantly life. These colors make people forget and forgive," tells Maa.

Note for Parents and Teachers

Holi is a Hindu festival of colors celebrated from time immemorial. Popular across the globe, it is celebrated at the end of winter season in India. It falls on the full moon day of the month of Phalguna of the Hindu lunisolar calendar, around February and March. This is the time when wheat harvest is at the peak of its maturity, and it is time to relax for farmers. People rejoice the arrival of spring and its beauty by throwing colors on each other and praying for a good harvest. Holi is a unique example of a community festival that strengthens social and cultural bonds. Besides being a celebration of nature, it is also a celebration of victory of good over evil. There are many rituals and stories behind this cheerful celebration that reflect science of human well-being, respect for nature, and care for human society. There is a multitude of ways in which Holi is celebrated across India and other countries, what is common is the festival brings cheer to all.

Fire Ritual

The festivities begin on the eve of the full moon day, also known as *Chhoti Holi* in Hindi. People light fire and gather around it to thank Mother Nature for taking care of all beings, to celebrate victory of virtues, and to bring good health during the change of season. They dance and sing to spread the message of love and friendship. They also pray and offer the first harvest to gods. They offer many medicinal substances like mustard seeds, sesame seeds, camphor, *yagya samagri*, dry cow dung cakes or *upalas*, into the fire and walk around it to destroy germs that grow more during this time of change in season. Among other substances, India's indigenous cow dung has proven benefits of cleaning the environment and protecting homes from harmful radiations and energies. Also, just by standing near such a fire, one feels energized and refreshed, it is aligned with *Bhuta Shuddhi*, a yogic practice of cleansing the fire element within one's body. This fire is also a symbol of victory of goodness over crime in our society and reminds one to speak up against anything wrong happening around them. Even though fire may cause destruction, when used in a controlled way it has helped farmers across the world to improve fertility of soil and make it possible for new crops to grow by clearing dead matter. For such reasons, many indigenous traditions across the world revere fire.

Playing with Colors

Colors heal the body and mind in different ways. When spring arrives, nature blesses us with colorful flowers. What nature gives is for a reason; it is for life to exist and prosper on the planet. Flowers are of immense importance across the world, any festival or ceremony is incomplete without flowers. They are symbols of hope, purity, love, and life. They not only make our lives more beautiful but also give birth to new plants, provide food to everyone, and have medicinal values. For this reason, several flowers find mention in many Sanskrit texts. Many Ayurvedic medicines and creams use specific flowers for their therapeutic properties. The most widely seen flower in Indian rituals is marigold, it has several skin healing properties. Many Indian desserts contain rose petals, as they are known for being an antidepressant as well. Palash flowers are widely used on Holi as they are a great skin cleanser. Besides flowers, many fruits, berries, trees' bark, and leaves are used to make Holi colors even more special and beneficial. Also, water splashing on Holi brings joy and heals our skin after a long, dark, and dry winter. Cool water has several health benefits in the system of Yoga, as it reenergizes us in many ways beyond superficial cleaning of the skin.

Messages of Holi

Several stories and descriptions of Holi are there in various Indian texts dating back hundreds of years. Prahlad's story tells us that no one is good or bad, privileged or backward by birth, it is one's actions and thoughts that define them. The stories of Putna and Dhondha caution us against danger and disease. The episode of visiting a farmer Maaloo is to kindle the spark of gratitude towards nature and our farmers, who work tirelessly to provide us with food. Here is a Sanskrit verse recognizing the role of farmers in our societies:

गणयन्ति न ये सूर्यं वृष्टिं शीतं च कर्षकाः ।
यतन्ते सस्यलाभाय तैः साकं हि वसामि अहं ॥
(ganayanti na ye suryam vristhim sheetam cha karshakah
yatante sasyalaabhaaya taih saakam hi vasaami aham)

It means, "The Divine always lives with those farmers who persistently work hard to grow crops without being bothered by Sun's heat, rain, and cold temperatures." Holi is a celebration of nature, agriculture, water, fire, love, friendship, life, and goodness. Let us wish a very Happy Holi, may colors of wellbeing, happiness, and harmony fill all lives.

Glossary

Agni uhg-nee Meaning, fire. Personified as a deity, *Agni Dev*. One of the five elements all beings are made of, known as *panch-maha-bhutas* in Yoga. This energy is what causes digestion and gives one the ability to think and achieve. Fire rituals like *Yagyas* bring well-being as specific medicinal substances are offered into fire with chanting of Sanskrit mantras.

Avatar uh-vuh-tahr When the divine is born on Earth, they are called *Avatar*. The Avatars of Lord Vishnu are also aligned with the evolution of life and human consciousness on Earth.

Badi Holi buh-dee hoh-lee Second day of Holi when people play with colors. *Badi* means big or the main day of Holi.

Chhoti Holi cchoh-tee hoh-lee Day before Holi, known as *Chhoti* (small) Holi, on this day people light bonfires to signify the burning of negative forces, illnesses, and enmity. This ritual is known as Holika Dahan (**hoh-li-kah duh-hun**).

Dahi vada duh-hee vuh-dah Fried lentil-flour balls soaked in yogurt, served with a sweet and sour dressing made with tamarind and jaggery.

Deva dhay-vuh Meaning, Deity. From Sanskrit root verb *Div*, meaning, to *shine*. One who exhibits godly qualities, also used to address someone with respect. *Devi* for women.

Dharma dhur-muh Righteousness, eternal law of conduct centred around life to ensure human well-being. It is free to evolve and is therefore conditioned by time and space/location.

Gujiya guu-JEE-yah A sweet deep-fried dumpling filled with shredded coconut, nuts, and raisins.

Guru guu-ruu A teacher, someone who shows us the right path to success, a guide, a mentor.

Himalaya hi-mah-luh-yuh *Him* means snow in Hindi and *alaya* means a dwelling. A mountain range, the abode of Lord Shiva and the source of the sacred river, Ganga.

Kansa KUHN-suh A cruel king, brother of Lord Krishna's mother, Devaki. He imprisoned Devaki and killed her six new-born babies. He did every possible thing to kill baby Krishna as well.

Krishna KRISH-nuh Avatar of Lord Vishnu, who gave knowledge and the messages of devotion, lawfulness, and action. One of the most charming Hindu deities worshipped in several forms across the world.

Maa MAH Mother.

Narasimha nuhr-si-muh *Nara* means human and *Simha* means a lion. This is one of the fiercest deities, an avatar of Vishnu, destroyer of injustice and persecution, personification of valor, strength, and courage, restorer of *Dharma*.

Palash puh-lah-shuh A tree native to India, gives vibrant flowers that have colors of flame. It is widely used to prepare colorful water to play Holi. It has medicinal values as well.

Pichkari pich-kah-ree Water gun used for playing Holi.

Prasad pruh-sah-dh A devotional offering made to a deity and later offered to devotees, it is of various types depending on the purpose of a ritual or deity, they may even be made in a way that they have medicinal values.

Radha rah-dhah Krishna's childhood friend, a goddess of devotion and success, light of compassion.

Thandaai thun-dah-ee A traditional milk-based drink packed with seeds and nuts, boosts immunity, relieves stress, and detoxifies body.

Upala oo-puh-lah Dried cow dung cakes used as fuel for fire rituals. India's indigenous cows' dung has several medicinal qualities and is therefore used even for sacred rituals.

Vishnu vish-noo Force that preserves the functioning of the universe and is present everywhere.

Yudhishthira yuu-dhih-sh-thi-ruh Upholder of *Dharma*, the eldest of the five heroic brothers mentioned in the Mahabharata. He became the King after the Mahabharata war and restored justice and peace in the Indian subcontinent with the guidance of Lord Krishna and support of his brothers and wife.

**Dedicated to all children who brighten up the world
with their joyfulness and cheer.**

ISBN: 978-1-953384-27-0 (e-book)
ISBN: 978-1-953384-26-3 (paperback)
ISBN: 978-1-953384-25-6 (hardcover)
Library of Congress Control Number: 2021952229

First edition 2022
Printed in China

Published by Eternal Tree Books LLC
East Brunswick, NJ, USA
www.eternaltreebooks.com

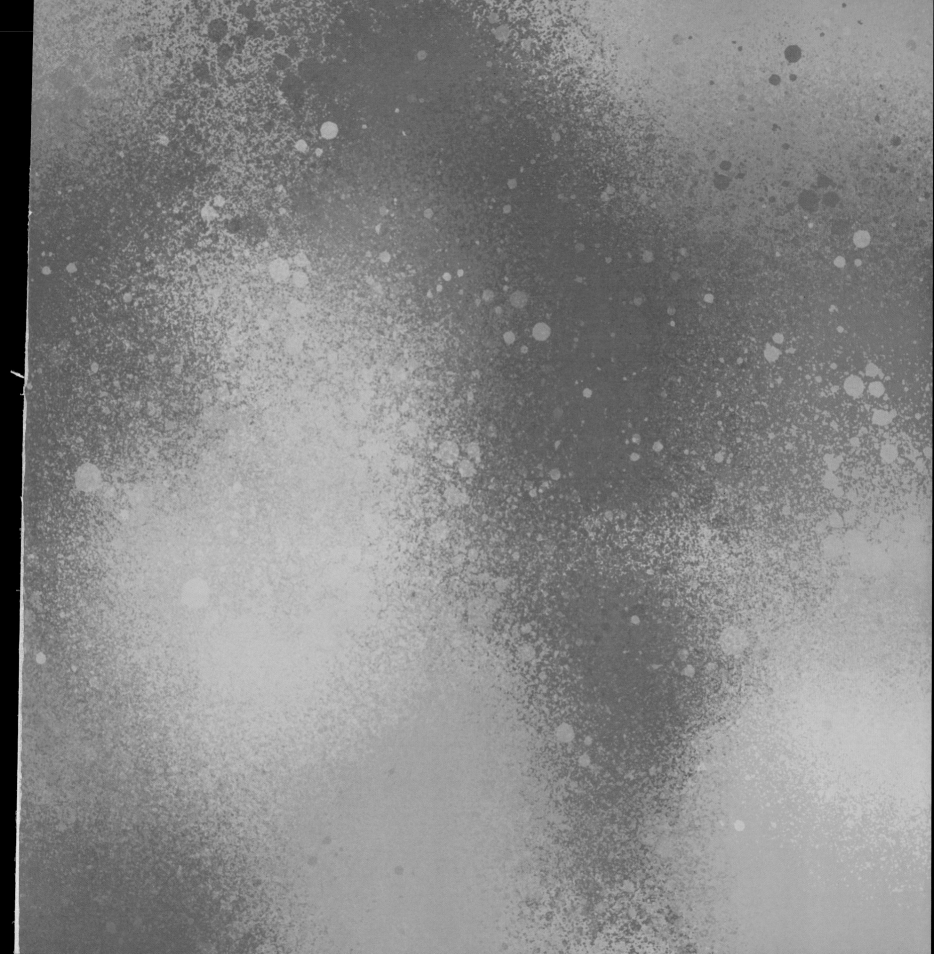